OAK TREE

WEBS OF LIFE

OAK TREE

Paul Fleisher

BENCHMARK BOOKS

MARSHALL CAVENDISH
NEW YORK

The author would like to acknowledge Paul Sieswerda of the New York Aquarium for his careful reading. The author also thanks his editor, Kate Nunn. And finally, he would like to thank his wife, Debra, for her support in all things, including the work on this book.

Benchmark Books
Marshall Cavendish Corporation
99 White Plains Road
Tarrytown, New York 10591-9001

Illustration by Jean Cassels

Library of Congress Cataloging-in-Publication Data
Fleisher, Paul.
Oak Tree / Paul Fleisher.
  p.   cm.—(Webs of Life.)
Includes bibliographic references (p.   ) and index.
Summary: Describes the role of an oak tree in the ecology of the Pennsylvania forest in which it lives.
ISBN 0-7614-0434-1
1. Oak—Juvenile literature. 2. Oak—Ecology—Juvenile literature. 3.Forest ecology—Juvenile literature.
[1. Forest ecology. 2. Ecology. 3. Oak. 4. Trees.] I. Title. II. Series: Fleisher, Paul. Webs of Life.
QK495.F14F58 1998   583'.46—dc21   96-39962   CIP   AC

Photo research by Ellen Barrett Dudley

Cover photo: The National Audubon Society Collection / Photo Researchers, Inc. / V.P. Weinland

The photographs in this book are used by permission and through the courtesy of: *Earth Scenes*: Wendy Neefus, 2, 35; Ted Levin, 13 (left); John Lemker, 21; Patti Murray, 27. *The National Audubon Society Collection/Photo Researchers, Inc.*: Michael P. Gadomski, 6-7, 24, 25; Ellan Young, 8-9, 10, 10-11, 11; Jeff Lepore, 12; Farrell Grehan, 13 (right); Ken Brate, 15, 28; Laurence Pringle, 16; James Dickinson, 17 (left); Gregory K. Scott, 17 (right); Maslowski Photo, 18; George E. Jones, 20; Mark Wilson, 23 (left); Jim Zipp, 26; Blair Seitz, 30; Stephen P. Parker, 31 (left); Harry Rogers, 33 (right); Robert E. Murowchick, 34. *Animals Animals*: Donald Specker, 14 (left), 33 (left); Joe McDonald, 19, 23 (right); Ted Levin, 22; Gary W. Griffen, 29; Z. Leszczynski, 31 (right). *Tom Stack & Associates*: D.G. Barker, 14 (right); Milton Rand, 32.

Printed in the United States of America

6 5 4 3 2 1

Dedicated to the memory of my uncle, Jack Fleisher

A great oak tree spreads its branches almost one hundred feet above the forest floor. Its leaves shade the ground below. Many creatures depend on the oak tree for food and shelter. This oak and the trees around it are at the center of a web of life.

There are many different kinds of oak trees. Oaks are one of the most important trees in the forests of the eastern United States. But they are not the only trees you'll find here. Look around. You'll see hickory trees, maples, beech trees, tulip trees, and others.

Four hundred years ago, the East was covered with woodlands.

Colonists from Europe cleared the forests to make farmland. They used the wood to build homes, boats, and furniture. And they burned the wood for fuel. Land that is forest today may have been a pasture or a plowed field in the 1800s.

Oak trees can live for four hundred years, but this oak is probably only about one hundred years old.

WHITE OAK, SUMMER

FALL

WINTER

Most trees in the eastern forest are deciduous. That means they lose their leaves each year. In the fall the leaves turn yellow, red, orange, and brown before they drop to the ground. In the winter, the woods are gray and bare.

Each spring the oak tree grows

SPRING

a new crop of young, green leaves. The leaves are green because of a substance called chlorophyll. All green plants have it. Chlorophyll uses the energy of sunlight to turn air and water into food. The tree uses the food to grow.

A few small plants
poke up through the leaves.
These beautiful pink lady's
slippers bloom each spring.
Please don't pick them.
They are very delicate.

LADY'S SLIPPERS

MOSS ON RED OAK

FIDDLE HEAD FERN

Thick mats of moss grow at the base of the tree. Young ferns unroll their lacy leaves. Ferns and moss grow best where the ground is damp. The shade and the cover of leaves help keep the ground beneath the tree moist.

13

EARTHWORM

RED SALAMANDER

Let's turn over the leaves to see what's living there. We might find an earthworm, digging its way through the leaves. And here's a red salamander, hunting earthworms for its next meal. Both the salamander and the worm stay hidden under the leaves to keep their skins moist.

Mice burrow beneath the leaves and twigs. If you look closely, you might see the pathways they've made.

WHITE-FOOTED MICE

CATERPILLAR

OAK APPLE GALL

By summer, the oak's branches support a canopy of leaves high above the ground. Many insects live on the leaves of the canopy. Caterpillars munch on the oak leaves. Later they will spin cocoons and change into moths or butterflies. Oak leaves are these caterpillars' favorite food.

A tiny wasp lays its eggs on a leaf. The leaf forms a round gall that protects the young wasp larva. After the wasp grows into an adult, you may find the gall lying on the forest floor. It looks like a brown golf ball.

The canopy is a home for larger creatures, too. A pair of gray squirrels have built their nest of leaves high up in the branches. The squirrels are raising their young in the nest. In the winter-time, the leaves help the squirrels stay warm and dry.

FEMALE GRAY SQUIRREL
NURSING

Listen. A woodpecker taps on a dying tree limb, searching for insects to eat. Woodpeckers also peck out larger holes for their nests. Many other birds, from little chickadees to great horned owls, also make their homes in this tree. In the spring and summer, the calls of birds and insects fill the air.

Some of the insects that live in the forest bite. Deerflies and mosquitos need a meal of animal blood before they can produce their eggs. When we walk through the forest in the spring or summertime, they may find us and bite us, too.

PILEATED WOODPECKER

Smaller trees and shrubs grow among the large oaks. This part of the forest is called the understory. The understory plants must survive in the shade of the big trees above them.

Holly is a common understory tree. Holly doesn't lose its leaves in the fall. It stays green all year long. Be careful. The shiny holly leaves have sharp, prickly spines.

HOLLY WITH BERRIES

Dogwood is another understory tree. In the spring, it has beautiful white flowers. Later, in the fall, birds will eat its bright red berries. Wild azaleas, blueberry bushes, and other shrubs also grow in the understory.

FLOWERING DOGWOOD

RACCOON
WITH
ACORN

If we're very still and quiet, we might see some of the animals that live near the oak. This raccoon makes its home in a hollow at the base of the tree. At night, it hunts for frogs, birds, and other small animals. Raccoons also eat eggs, berries, and almost anything else they can find.

White-tailed deer also live in the forest. They find most of their food at the edges of the woods and in the open fields nearby.

BLACK RAT SNAKE

Black snakes are excellent climbers. We might see one climbing the tree. The snake is searching for a bird's nest, where it can find eggs or young birds to eat.

WHITE-TAILED BUCK

This curly, gray-green material growing on the bark of the tree is called lichen. Lichen is actually two living things growing together—algae and fungus. Like any plant, the algae makes food using air, water, and sunlight. The fungus clings firmly to the tree to give the algae solid support. In return, the fungus shares the algae's food.

Around the tree, the forest floor is covered with a thick, springy blanket of fallen leaves and twigs. Plants that live on the forest floor must be able to survive with little light. Almost no direct sunlight reaches the ground.

LICHEN

In the fall, the leaves of the oak stop making food. They dry out and turn from green to brown. The leaves drop off and drift down to deepen the blanket of litter on the forest floor.

Insects, fungi, and bacteria digest and decompose the dead leaves. Slowly, the leaves turn into soil. After a heavy rain, stemmed fungi called mushrooms push their way through the cover of leaves. Don't touch! Some forest mushrooms are very poisonous.

The mushrooms release millions of spores. The tiny seed-like spores float away on the wind. Perhaps they will grow into new fungi in another part of the forest.

PUFFBALL
FUNGUS
RELEASING
SPORES

MUSHROOMS
GROWING FROM
DEAD OAK

BLUE JAY

Each fall the oak produces thousands of acorns. Many forest creatures depend on these nuts for food. Squirrels and blue jays harvest some of them even before they fall.

Wild turkeys look for acorns that have fallen to the ground. The male turkey—the gobbler—has an especially beautiful display of feathers. Deer, mice, and other forest creatures eat the acorns all winter long.

Every few years, oak trees produce an especially large crop of acorns. These years are called mast years. During mast years, there is extra food for animals to eat, so there are usually more wild creatures living in the forest.

28

Years from now, this great oak tree will weaken and die. A gust of wind from a powerful summer storm may bring it crashing down. But even after it dies, the tree will provide food and homes for many forest creatures.

FROG EGGS

SPRING PEEPER

Rain may form a temporary pond where the tree was uprooted. Green algae will grow in the still water. Frogs, salamanders, mosquitoes, and other creatures will lay their eggs in the water. Soon the tiny pond will be full of tadpoles and wiggling insect larvae.

CENTIPEDE

Termites and ants will burrow through the wood. Centipedes, spiders, and other small predators will live in the rotting log, too.

Pill bugs will also live in the dead tree. Pill bugs are not insects. They are related to shrimp and crabs. Pill bugs have a hard outer

PILL BUG . . .

. . . ROLLED UP IN DEFENSE

shell. If you pick one up, it protects itself by rolling into a ball.

Insects, bacteria, and fungi will digest the wood of the fallen tree and turn it back into soil. Seeds will sprout and grow on rotting wood. The old tree will slowly disappear into the forest floor.

SPROUTING ACORN

Meanwhile, when the tree falls, it will leave a large open space in the forest canopy. Bright sunlight will now reach the ground. Acorns that a squirrel or other animal buried will sprout and grow. The oak seedlings will reach up toward the light. And after many years, one little seedling will grow as big and tall as the old oak that once stood here, so long ago.

Can you name the plants and animals around this oak tree?
Turn the page to check your answers.

Plants and Animals Around This Oak Tree

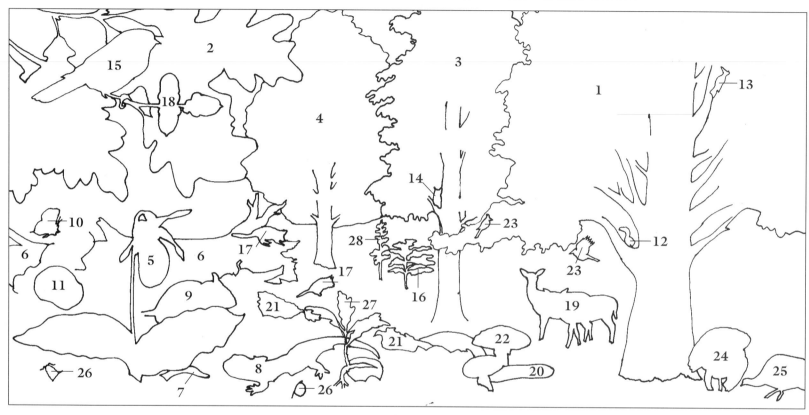

1. white oak
2. white oak leaf
3. hickory
4. maple
5. lady's slipper
6. moss
7. earthworm

8. red salamander
9. white-footed mouse
10. butterfly
11. oak apple gall
12. squirrel
13. pileated woodpecker
14. owl

15. chickadee
16. dogwood
17. raccoon
18. acorn
19. white-tailed deer
20. black rat snake
21. lichen

22. mushroom
23. blue jay
24. male turkey
25. female turkey
26. pill bug
27. oak seedling
28. young oak

FIND OUT MORE

Behm, Barbara. *Exploring Woodlands.* Milwaukee, WI: Gareth Stevens, 1994.

Greenaway, Theresa. *Tree Life.* New York: Dorling Kindersley, 1992.

Hankin, Rosie. *Up the Tall Tree.* Chatham, NJ: Raintree Steck-Vaughn, 1995.

Hirschi, Ron. *Faces in the Forest.* New York: Cobblehill, 1996.

Owen, Oliver S. *Acorn to Oak Tree.* Minneapolis, MN: Abdo & Daughters, 1994.

Thornhill, Jan. *A Tree in a Forest.* New York: Simon & Schuster, 1992.

INDEX

ABOUT THE AUTHOR

In addition to writing children's books, Paul Fleisher teaches gifted middle school students in Richmond, Virginia. He spends many hours outdoors, gardening or fishing on the Chesapeake Bay. Fleisher's back porch looks out on a shady oak forest full of deer, squirrels, turkeys, and other wild creatures.

Fleisher is also active in organizations that work for peace and social justice, including the Richmond Peace Education Center and the Virginia Forum.